THE FIRST BOOK OF CAVES

BY ELIZABETH HAMILTON

PICTURES BY BETTE J. DAVIS

FRANKLIN WATTS
NEW YORK

Copyright© 1956 by Franklin Watts, Inc.

Printed in the United States of America
Published in Canada by Ambassador Books, Ltd., Toronto 1, Ontario
Library of Congress Catalog Card Number: 54-9818
FOURTH PRINTING

NEW WORLDS TO EXPLORE ⬎ UNDERGROUND

One November day in the year 1879 a little five-year-old girl, Maria de Sautuola, was playing in a cave near her home in Altamira, Spain. She often went to this cave with her father, who liked to collect the rough tools of stone and bone that had been left there by ancient men thousands of years before.

Finding the tools was slow work, and on this particular day Maria grew tired watching her father scrape about in the dust of the cave's floor. She lay down and looked drowsily around. She loved the soft darkness and the strange twists and turns of the walls. As she lay with her candle beside her, watching its wavering light, she suddenly noticed something—something high above her on

1

the cave's ceiling. It was an enormous red picture of an animal that looked like a bull. In the flickering light it seemed almost to move. She flashed her candle into another corner. A second beast appeared.

"Father! Father!" she shouted. "Bulls! Bulls!"

As her father turned, she pointed to the paintings, but he could see nothing.

"Don't you see them, father? There, and there!" Again she pointed to the big, bright drawings.

At last he made them out—huge, bulky animals painted in vivid colors upon the rocky cave walls and ceiling. Ex-

citedly he looked, and the more he looked the more animals he saw—strange creatures not quite like any that he knew.

Gradually, as he studied them in the days that followed, he understood what they were. Here were beasts which had roamed the earth twenty thousand years before. Ancient hunters of those times—who were great artists, too—had painted these animals deep within the cave. On the walls were pictures of galloping horses, deer, wild boars, and fierce bison.

As the years went by, more ancient cave pictures were

3

found. One of the most interesting discoveries was in Lascaux, France. There, in the year 1940, four boys were walking across a field, as they often did. With them was their pet dog. Suddenly he disappeared as if he had dropped into the earth. They shouted and whistled, but the dog did not come. They looked and looked, but still no dog. Then at last they found the answer to the puzzle: there, beside a bush, was a small hole. The dog really had dropped into the earth. Down they went after him, and found themselves in a deep cave. One of them had a flashlight. Immediately they started to explore. Almost at once their flashlight showed them stags and herds of horses painted on the walls and on the ceiling. They had discovered one of the earliest and most impressive of all the known caves of the ancient hunters.

4

Today visitors to France and Spain flock to look at the cave paintings discovered by children. Although these wonderful paintings were made thousands of years ago by primitive men, long before civilization, the drawings of mammoths, deer, woolly rhinoceroses, fish, and other creatures are some of the finest art of all time. But strangely, when people are pictured they do not look like people at all. They are drawn with stiff, straight lines, and scientists call them "stick" people because they look like twigs.

That is in the caves of Europe. In Australia it is different. People drawn in the Australian caves are blocked out in huge figures with eyes and noses, but never any mouths! The Australian drawings were made about ten thousand years ago. Like those in Europe they picture animals wonderfully: fish, crocodiles, and whales—creatures

5

men who live by the sea would know.

From the ancient cave pictures, students have learned much about prehistoric times. Flat stones have been found on which bright-colored clays were mixed with grease to make paints. Rough brushes and hollow bone tubes for blowing color onto walls have been discovered. Stone lamps like dishes, found lying in the caves, must once have been lighted by moss wicks floating in animal fat. The pictures themselves are of animals the artists must often have seen and come to know well. Many of the creatures no longer exist.

Many things about these pictures are not known, however. Why were they drawn in caves far underground where there is no light? How were the artists able to reach high enough to make the paintings far up on the walls and to paint those that are on the ceilings? Often one animal has been drawn on top of another. Why? Some of the animal pictures look as if stones had been thrown at them. Was this to put a spell on beasts that the artists expected to hunt? Was it to teach young hunters to aim well? Or was it for some unguessed religious reason? Why are people drawn in such strange ways, looking like sticks in Europe, and bulky and mouthless in Australia?

Caves have many such secrets, and we are only now beginning to learn some of them. In the underground world there is much that is still waiting to be discovered. Today many people are becoming cave explorers. In caves scientists are finding interesting new things about the earth and about the rocks, the plants, the animals, and people of long ago, as well as of today. And in caves plain ordinary folks are discovering adventure and a thrilling hobby. Scientists who study caves are called speleologists (spee-lee-OL-oh-jists)—a name that comes from the Greek word *spelaion*, which means cave. And people who explore caves for fun have a name for themselves, too—spelunkers, from *spelunca*, the Latin word for cave. They are also called cavers.

Wind cave

HOW CAVES ARE MADE

All over the earth there are caves—hollow spaces underground. A cave may be one chamber or a series of connected spaces, but no matter how large or small it is, in order to be a true cave it must have been made by nature. You may dig a hole deep into the side of a hill and you may call it a cave, but it is not a true cave. Only underground holes that are made naturally, and not by animals or human beings, are true caves.

There are five principal kinds of caves: wind caves, wave caves, lava caves, ice caves, and limestone caves.

Wind caves are made in mountainsides where the wind

blows almost without stopping. Here small pieces of grit and sand are swept along with such force that they finally grind deep hollows into soft spots in the rock, almost as if a huge giant had rubbed away the caves with sandpaper.

Wave caves are made in seaside cliffs by waves beating against soft places and gradually wearing large holes. Wave caves are often called sea caves, but there is another kind of sea cave that is found *under* the water. Divers report that underwater hollows are wonderful places filled with strange fish and beautiful sea plants. Few spelunkers are deep-sea divers, however, and when they speak of sea caves they usually mean wave caves.

Lava caves are made in still a different way. Lava is the melted liquid rock which pours from an active vol-

Wave cave

cano. As it flows away from the volcano it cools and hardens. First it becomes solid on the surface, though it may still be soft underneath. Sometimes the soft liquid lava bursts out at the end of the flow and runs from under the hardened crust. The tunnel-like hollow which is left is called a lava cave.

Ice caves are made entirely of ice. They are found in glaciers where it is terribly cold, in the Arctic and Antarctic areas or in mountainous regions of everlasting snow, such as the high Pyrenees in Spain, or the Alps in Switzerland. These ice caves are very beautiful, with frozen waterfalls, huge icicles so clear that they can be seen through, and lovely ice crystals, all in shining blue and green colors like those of the glass mountains of fairy tales. Ice caves are very slippery, of course, and they are likely to have cold winds blowing through them. Then too they are constantly melting and refreezing in new shapes.

Some other caves which are not made entirely of ice, but where ice forms, are also called ice caves. Cave ice is, like all ice, just frozen water. Cave ice was used at a long-ago banquet given by the French king Francis I, who was a spelunker himself. This happened about fifty years after

10

Ice cave

Columbus discovered America. It was not until many, many years later that ice boxes made it possible for everyone to have ice, and ice cream, in even the hottest weather.

The largest and most numerous caves of all, however, are those made of limestone, a soft, chalklike rock which lies in thick layers over many parts of the earth. When limestone cracks, it splits up and down as well as sideways. Limestone also dissolves easily. Caves are formed as a result of these two things: cracking and the wearing away which follows, and dissolving. In both cases water is the chief worker in making limestone caves.

Water goes down through the soil or through any crack in rock, seeping and oozing steadily farther under the earth. Often, as it filters downward, water joins with another substance that helps it to go down through the limestone. From the air and soil, water picks up a gas, carbon dioxide, which mixes with it to make an acid. This acid liquid seeps down through the earth, dissolving the limestone faster than pure water can. Finally it reaches the water table, the top of the layer of water which lies under the earth's surface. Or it may reach a layer of rock like sandstone or shale, which an acid cannot affect. When the water reaches the layer of rock which it cannot go through, it moves slowly sideways, eating away the limestone and sometimes forming a series of underground chambers. If the hard layers of rock change their position or if the underground layer of water is lowered, empty chambers are left, and then streams may begin to flow through them.

Grit, fine sand, pebbles, or even small rocks may be collected by underground streams and pushed along. They rub against the sides of the passageways, widen cracks in the limestone, and carry some bits of limestone along with them. Whole streams take part in this wearing-away process. Countless years later they dry up; or in wearing deep channels they leave their old beds empty—and open, dry caves are left where rivers once ran.

It takes thousands and thousands of years for caves to form; they are not made quickly. As long as water seeps into them they keep growing and changing and are called "live" caves. A cave without water is a "dead" cave; it can-

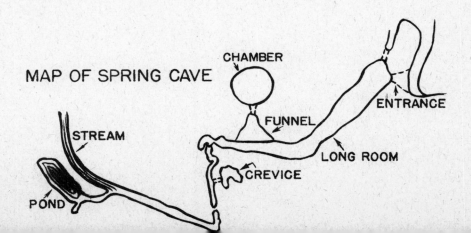

MAP OF SPRING CAVE

not change any more except as parts of its ceilings and walls collapse.

Most caves are live. They are damp and some of them have streams and rivers flowing through them; or they may contain pools or even large underground lakes. In many caves, water oozes out of the ceilings and walls all the time, dripping down to the floor and often making a covering of sticky mud that is cold and soft and that clings like glue.

Often strange shapes called cave formations are made as water drips from the walls and ceilings. No two of these formations are ever alike, so no two caves are alike and each one is strange and exciting.

If you put a handful of salt into a cup of water it will dissolve. But when the water evaporates, the salt is left and will appear again. Something like this happens in limestone caves. Acid water oozing through the limestone into the cave carries with it calcium carbonate, or limestone, which it has dissolved from the rock as it seeped through. When this water strikes the air of the cave it starts to evaporate. This leaves a thick ooze of calcium carbonate, or limestone. Some of it falls in drops to the floor and some stays clinging to the ceiling. Finally the

14

water evaporates entirely, and limestone is left, in the way that salt was left in the cup. This limestone makes cave formations. The material that stays clinging to the ceiling looks something like a tiny icicle and grows in much the same way. These stone "icicles" are called stalactites (sta-LAK-tites). Some stalactites are enormous, but they form very slowly, often growing only about an inch in a hundred years. As they become longer they also grow bulkier, because water dripping down them leaves limestone on their sides.

Not all the limy water clings to the ceiling, however. Some of the solution drops to the floor, where more of the water evaporates. The limestone on the ground piles up in a formation called a stalagmite (sta-LAG-mite). Stalagmites rise from the ground in many different shapes.

Some of them look like many-layered birthday cakes, some like mushrooms several stories high, and some like icicles upside down.

Stalactites and stalagmites are easy to tell apart, and their names are easy to remember; a stalactite—the one that contains the letter c—clings tightly to the c-eiling; a stalagmite—the one that contains the letter g—grows from the g-round. Both of these words come from the Greek language and mean "oozing out in drops" and "dripping." That is exactly what stalactites and stalagmites are—drops and drips.

Sometimes a stalactite and a stalagmite grow so long that they meet and form a column. A row of stalactites may join sideways to make a beautiful formation called a drapery. Or water dripping along a very narrow crack may make a curtain.

17

Helictite

In some caves, drops of water with calcium carbonate in solution have left straight, slender, hollow stalactites. In other caves, queer formations called helictites (HEL-ik-tites) grow. They start like very thin stalactites, but suddenly shoot off at odd, unbelievable angles or even grow back up to the ceiling in airy, delicate patterns. No one is exactly sure why they take such strange turns and twists.

In some cave chambers that are airtight, rare formations called anthodites are found. Their name comes from the Greek word *anthos,* which means flower. They are well named, for they look like lovely white flowers growing in thick masses from the cave ceiling. Water seeps very slowly through tiny spaces in the rock to form their magical petals—delicate, hair-

18

like white spikes of limestone far different from the bulkier stalagmites that are also made of limestone.

In caves where there is gypsum, formations called gypsum flowers sometimes grow on the ceiling in beautiful white shapes that look like tiger lilies and rosettes. They too are formed by water seeping through the rock.

Certain minerals dissolved from the earth and rock through which the water seeps often tint cave drippings in a variety of colors. In some caves water flowing down the walls or dripping from the ceiling produces a formation in alternate dark and light stripes. Because the colored bands make it look a little like a slice of bacon, this formation is called "bacon" or "bacon strip."

19

Anthodite

Gypsum flower

Cave pearls are sometimes found in pools on the floors. They grow around tiny grains of sand in the pools, which are constantly churned about by dripping water. Gradually the grains take on a coating of lime which grows thicker and thicker until little white pearl-like balls are made. These cave pearls may grow to be about as big as a sparrow's egg.

Sometimes slowly flowing water leaves formations that look like stone waterfalls. It is amazing that minerals dissolved in dripping water can take so many different forms and have so many different colors. They help make caves interesting and exciting places.

INSIDE OF CAVES

No two caves are alike, and cavers are never sure just what they will find in one that has never before been explored. Even cave entrances, or mouths, differ one from another. Some slope gradually into the ground, while others go down very suddenly and steeply, and still others are straight up-and-down shafts in which explorers must use a ladder. Some mouths are huge and yawning, as is that of Nickajack Cave in Tennessee, which is 175 feet wide and 60 feet high. On the other hand, some of the largest caves have such small, narrow mouths that cavers must squeeze into them by crawling on their hands and knees.

Carlsbad Caverns in New Mexico is one of the largest caves in the United States. It is known to extend at least 25 miles. One of its rooms, far below the earth's surface, is 4,000 feet long, more than 600 feet wide, and at one point is 300 feet high. It could hold more than twenty baseball fields. Yet this cave went unnoticed for many years. It was finally discovered by a cowboy, who, when he was riding across the plains, saw what he thought was smoke coming out of the ground. He hurried to investigate, and found that the "smoke" was a huge column of many thousands of bats flying out of the cave's tiny entrance.

Perhaps the most exciting entrances of all are those of some of the wave caves, which must often be entered by boat. It is a wonderful experience to float into a wave cave with its great rocks arching overhead. Some of the caves can be entered only at low tide, and then only if the sea is calm.

Just off the coast of Scotland, on the island of Staffa in the Hebrides, is Fingal's Cave. It can be approached only by drifting under an entrance arch towering sixty feet overhead. The musician Felix Mendelssohn came to this cave when he was a young man. He was so impressed

both by the cave itself and by the sound of the winds and the waves echoing through it that he wrote, there in the cave, several bars of a piece of music. He later finished it and called it *Fingal's Cave Suite, The Hebrides Overture*. Today it is a well-known piece of music which symphony orchestras play.

The air in most caves is pure and pleasant. Some caves have currents of air blowing through them just as breezes do aboveground.

Temperatures differ from cave to cave, although year in and year out the temperature in each particular cave re-

23

mains almost the same — about like that of the average temperature aboveground in that area. So, if a cave is in a region that is always cold and snowy, its temperature will never be above freezing. And if a cave is near the hot equator it will never be cool inside. But the unchanging temperature will be most noticeable in places which have hot summers and cold winters. Inside a cave in this type of climate the temperature will vary only a few degrees. Therefore in summer it will seem cool and in winter it will seem warm. Because of their steady, rather cool temperature, such caves are wonderful places in which to keep perishable food. Even the United States Government has used caves for storing food surpluses.

Caves are usually silent places. The dripping water in them makes soft, pleasant noises, but these are the only sounds unless some visitor disturbs the quiet. Some caves are shaped so that they have wonderful echoes in them, while others, of different shape, have no echoes at all. Many hundreds of years ago ancient priests called druids used the echoes of a cave in France to make their voices sound louder. This cave was probably one of the first loud-speaking systems.

Many small caves are not very deep, so that they always have some light in them. But away from the mouth of a cave it soon gets dark. The English playwright Shakespeare could have been thinking of a cave when he wrote: "Time must have a stop." In caves, time really does seem to stop. One year is like the next year. There is little sound, no time, and no weather.

If cave explorers put out their lights, they are in total darkness, which is quite different from night darkness. The darkness in a cave is a complete lack of light — ten times darker than when your eyes are shut outdoors at night. The blackness seems to make more clear the sound of water dripping — dripping in many caves without ever stopping. Cave darkness makes explorers more aware of the air moving around them. As they stand there, a feeling of wonder comes over them to think of this cave so far from the everyday world — this cave silently and slowly growing and changing, with the water forever building and destroying. Here, in the pitch-black darkness, the cave creatures—snails, salamanders, insects, and fish— noiselessly live out their lives.

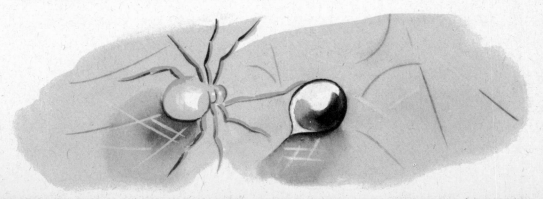

ANIMALS THAT LIVE IN CAVES

A surprising variety of animals are found in caves. Some — the true cave creatures — stay underground all their lives without ever going up to the surface. But other creatures live in caves only part of the time. Bears, foxes, raccoons, weasels, hyenas, jackals, and some kinds of mice are among the animals who spend most of their time aboveground and find their food there. However, they often use caves when they want to get away from the sun or rain, raise their families, or just take a nap. Some of them den up in small natural caves during the cold winters of northern climates.

Other animals spend most of their lives in caves. Among them are many members of the bat family. They are halfway between the true cave animals and those who live underground for only a small part of the time. Bats are found in most parts of the world. Although all of them fly, they are mammals: that is, instead of hatching from eggs, their young are born as are those of other furry, four-legged animals, and they are fed with milk from their mothers' breasts. Instead of feathers, bats' bodies are covered with fur. Their wings are made of thin skin which stretches between the long fingers of their front limbs and along their sides. Bats hang upside down in hollow trees and in cracks and crevices in old buildings or caves. Their feet are shaped for hanging rather than walking. They are not blind, but the light of day probably hurts their weak eyes. Most of them sleep in the daytime and fly in the twilight or at night to find their food. Some tropical bats eat fruit; a few catch fish while they skim over the surface of the water; and two kinds in the American tropics drink the blood of other animals. But most bats eat insects.

Caves are perfect places for bats to sleep during the daytime. Sometimes they live in huge colonies. There is one large cave in which it is thought that between 20 or 30 million of them live and sleep peacefully together. In the daytime the ceiling of this cave is a mass of bats, hanging in great furry mats. At twilight, when the animals fly out in a steady procession for their evening meal of insects, four hours go by before the outward parade is ended.

It is amazing that, although bats fly in and out through small spaces at a rate of about thirty miles an hour, they never seem to have a traffic jam or an accident. This is because each animal has a remarkable natural radar system. As he flies, a bat keeps making small cries — about fifty of them a second. These are pitched so high that a human being cannot hear them. But a bat can hear them, and he hears the echoes that bounce off objects in his way, just as if he had a radar set. This is called echo location. By his constant tuning in on these bouncing sound waves a bat can judge how far he is from something in his path, and he changes his course to fly around it.

The South American oilbirds, brownish-gray creatures with a wingspread of almost four feet, also live in caves and leave them only after dark. Deep in the cave blackness these birds make their nests of clay. Like the bat they have weak eyes and almost useless feet, but they can fly for long distances. They are believed to travel as far as 130 miles in one night in search of certain fruit and nuts.

Besides these creatures, certain kinds of crayfish, frogs, and insects like dark caves. These particular species spend most of their lives underground, and go out only once in a while, to catch food or go exploring.

Salamanders live in many places. Some never leave the water, and others never leave the woods. Still others spend part of their lives in one place and part in another. However, all salamanders must live in cool, damp surroundings. Since they have very small lungs — and some kinds have no lungs at all — they breathe through their skins. They cannot do this unless they keep their skins moist.

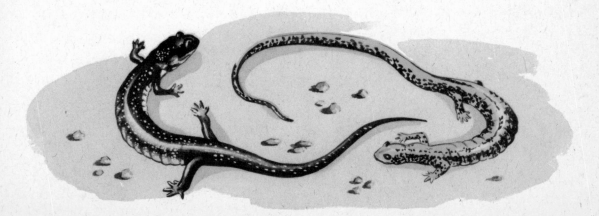

The zigzag salamander is one that lives in the woods for a part of its life and in caves for the rest of the time. It is purplish-gray in color, has a zigzag stripe down its back, and has bulging eyes like those of many night hunters and lovers of the dark. Not a great deal is known about its life, but we do know that the young zigzags are raised in caves, where the eggs have sometimes been found. They are covered with a thinner jellylike coat than are frogs' eggs. And instead of laying her eggs in water as a frog does, the mother salamander glues them together, hiding them in a crack or crevice of a damp cave.

During the three months before hatching time, either the mother or the father salamander stays curled around the eggs, or close to them. The eggs must be watched all the time because other salamanders and cave creatures are always ready to eat them. Besides this, mold grows very quickly on the eggs, and would prevent them from hatching if it were not removed. We do not know how the

30

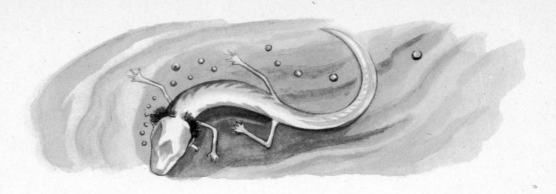

parent salamander carries out his difficult baby-sitting job, but it is likely that he licks off the mold as it forms.

In America there are two kinds of blind salamanders which have been found living in caves. One of them, the *Typhlomolge* (tif-lo-MOL-gee), found only in Texas, never leaves the water. He has no way of breathing except with leatherlike gills which open on the outside of his body. These gills are fringed and are a beautiful bright red, while the rest of him is pure, pearly white. He looks as fragile as if he were made of glass. Even if he could breathe out of water, his thin spindly legs are so weak that they could not hold him up on land. With the water to buoy up his body, however, he can walk rapidly and can even run along the streambeds. When he is in a great hurry he swims, keeping his legs close to his body and using his tail as a fish does, to drive himself forward. The eggs of the *Typhlomolge* have not yet been found. *Typhlo-*

molge is a true cave creature: that is, one that never leaves his underground home.

Among other true cave creatures are some kinds of worms, insects, snails, crayfish, and fish. These animals live always in darkness and have never seen the sunlight.

Sight is of no use to true cave animals, and most of them have lost the power of seeing. Some have no eyes, and some have eyes over which skin has grown. Cave creatures' senses of hearing, smell, and touch are especially keen, however, and help to make up for their blindness. Some of them have unusually long feelers, and some have long hairs which help in finding their way around in the dark.

True cave animals are silent, spooky creatures, white or very pale in color. One kind of shrimp, found in a pool far underground, is so colorless that it was not discovered until its shadow was seen moving across the bottom of

32

the pool. It is hard for us to imagine creatures so pale that their shadows are easier to see than the actual animals.

Some of the cave fish are almost as difficult to see, and are quite rare. One kind of Mexican blind cave fish is not hard to see and is no longer rare, however. It can be bought in a pet shop for less than a dollar. Those for sale in shops do not come from caves, but are bred in tropical fish farms. They are hardy little fish about three inches long—silvery white, with only two tiny sunken places remaining to show the former location of their eyes. They live to be about seven years old, and appear to be unaffected by the bright daylight of a glass aquarium, although it is certainly a change from the dark underground streams that their ancestors knew.

Cave crickets are pale creatures with very long feelers, three or four times the length of their bodies. They have eyes, but have little use for them. They are really mem-

33

bers of the katydid family, although they are silent and do not have the familiar song of the katydids that most of us know.

Cave beetles are completely blind and have no wings. They have long feelers which help them to find their way around. Among the many other kinds of cave insects are daddy-long-legs, springtails, and flies.

34

(Insects enlarged)

Some kinds of spiders and several kinds of flatworms are also cave dwellers. In New Zealand there is even one kind of thread-shaped insect larva or "worm" that glows like a light. Closely packed colonies of these worms hang from the ceilings of the famous Waitomo caverns and give enough light to read by. But they are easily frightened, and at the faintest sound they lose their brightness as though a light had been turned off.

All these creatures find their food in caves; they eat cave plants, bat guano, or other cave animals, or pick up morsels that are carried in by streams. Their dark, silent life is a strange one, but many of them, if they were taken aboveground, would quickly die. They are used to the darkness and even temperature of caves, and they would not be able to bear the daylight or the sudden shifts from hot to cold on the surface of the earth.

CAVE PLANTS

Although there are many astonishing cave animals, there are very few plants. Green plants cannot live where there is no light. Deep inside of caves, therefore, there are usually only non-green plants: tiny bacteria too small to be seen, and the very simple growths of the fungus family, like molds and mushrooms, which can live in darkness. Nearer the entrances, where dim light enters, mosses and tiny plants called algae are found. And close to the openings of caves, where there are light and dampness and proper temperature, thick clusters of beautiful ferns often decorate the rocks.

One strange, rare moss called *Schistostega osmundacea* (shis-to-STEE-ga os-mun-DA-se-a) likes the dark crevices. It is not a true green, and it is seldom noticed because ordinarily it looks like nothing but sticks or stones or mud. But suddenly, when a ray of light strikes it from just the right angle, it has a golden-green glow like a cat's eyes in the dark. Although it has no brightness of its own, a part of it reflects light just as a roadside reflector does. When light strikes it, it leaps into brilliance. You may have read in fairy tales about the pot of gold which the leprechauns buried. If a human being finally succeeds in finding the pot of fairy gold, it turns to dirt in his hands. The story is thought to have started with this strange moss which is sometimes dull, sometimes shining.

In some tropical caves, forests of tiny white or yellow trees grow from cocorite palm seeds dropped by oilbirds or fruit-eating bats. Aboveground the palms grow to majestic, green-leaved trees, but in the caves they are pale, eighteen-inch dwarfs.

Many people who grow food have discovered that caves can be valuable to them in their business. Commercial mushroom growers sometimes use caves as mushroom farms, because mushrooms are members of the fungus family which like the dark. Then too, vegetables like celery, chicory, and endive, that need to be bleached before they are marketed, are sometimes set out in flat boxes in caves. There they soon lose their green color.

PEOPLE WHO LIVE IN CAVES

Men have always been fascinated by caves, and they have also used them as homes. People who live in caves are called troglodytes (TROG-lo-dites) from a Greek word that means "one who creeps into holes."

In France today there are many troglodytes — indeed whole villages of them. Roche l'Eveque, in the valley of the Loir River, is a troglodyte town which has been occupied for as long as anyone can remember. The cave dwellers are ordinary people — farmers, winegrowers and tradesmen — who happen to prefer living in caves to living in houses. Over the years the troglodytes have "improved" their caves — that is, they have put in windows, doors, and other things to make their homes comfortable. At first glance the troglodytes' houses do not even appear to be caves. They are in the face of a cliff, and the cave-dwellers have built house fronts onto them. But the back walls and roofs are provided by the cave.

At Haute-Isle, near Paris, there is another such colony of people who have made their caves homelike and attractive. Their ancestors lived there, and each generation has made its own improvements. Perhaps Grandfather dug out another room, or made a hole and put in a window. Father may have added the storeroom and built a fireplace. The chimney, of course, went up through the ceiling, and that may have made a problem. For troglodytes must be careful when they make a hole in the roof that it  does not spoil the vegetable garden. For, after all, the roof is the ground!

The people of Haute-Isle also have an underground church. Its belfry sticks up above the earth like some queer little playhouse.

40

Some of the gypsy people in Spain are troglodytes. They, too, simply prefer to live in caves. In Asia, also, thousands of people live in this way.

The best known of the North American cave dwellers lived in the western part of our country many years ago. They must have arrived in prehistoric times — long before there was any written history. In various canyons they often used wind-carved caves, sometimes building their towns under the cliffs. These places were safe from hostile tribes, as they could be reached only by ladders which the people pulled up after them. Today some of these prehistoric settlements have been preserved as national parks, and they are fascinating places to visit.

In Bat Cave, New Mexico, corn, or maize, has been found that was left by inhabitants as long ago as 4,000 B.C. Mesa Verde National Park, in southwestern Colorado, has some of the country's most puzzling ancient cliff dwellings. Here are about 350 cliff dwellings, 400 pueblos on the top of the cliffs, and several hundred pit dwellings made by the early Basket Makers. At one place at Mesa Verde there is a great Cliff Palace placed in a cave. Many mysteries surround the cliffs and cave here. Scientists know that people lived here for nearly 1,800 years. As early as 500 B.C. and until about 1276 A.D. men lived in these caves. At one time 70,000 persons must have lived at Mesa Verde. It appears that the dwellings were deserted very suddenly. Around the year 1276 a terrible drought began in that area. Scientists believe that the dry weather drove the people from their dwellings, but to this day no one knows where they went. However, the dwellings still remain — remarkable and ghostly reminders of a long-ago people.

All through time and all over the world men have lived in caves, although many early people stayed only near the entrances. The deep darkness farther back was frightening to them, and they never explored it. Much of our knowledge of prehistoric men has come from study of the caves where they lived, but as with cave paintings, there are many unanswered questions about these early people.

In caves, scientists have found many clues as to how human beings may first have developed. In 1927, in a cave near Peking, China, a scientist found a tooth that was very ancient, but looked human. He believed that it belonged to a very early, primitive kind of man, whom he called Peking man. Further digging in the caves near Peking brought forth more bones, and more information about this very early, rather apelike man. Although Peking man was not very much like today's human beings, he did use tools — very roughly made stone choppers — and he knew how to use fire. Tools and several hearths were found in the caves.

In Europe many caves have contained the bones of Neanderthal (ne-AN-der-tal) men. Neanderthal men were one kind of primitive men. Indeed, in spots all over the world the bones of early men have been found in caves.

To a scientist, digging down through the dirt on a cave floor is often like turning the pages of history. The cave may have been inhabited by many people over thousands and thousands of years. Many a dweller in the cave left something behind: stone axes, flint tools, weapons, cooking utensils, bone needles, animal bones, perhaps even the seeds of grain he used as food. As the material became buried in the dust, it formed layers. Digging through them, a scientist can read each layer as if it were a chapter in a history book. But he reads the last part of the story first, because the most recently made layer is on the top.

In caves of the Near East, scientists believe they have found proof that here lived the first farmers in the world. They have found very old flint sickles with blades that have a queer shine. Grain-producing grasses contain a material called silica, which gives this same shine to flint blades used in reaping. Scientists believe these shiny blades prove that here lived very early men who grew grains and harvested them. This was the first farming in the whole world. In caves, scientists are continually finding thrilling clues that add to our knowledge.

CAVES FOR EVERYONE

Not only scientists, but all of us, can visit caves, for there are many tourist caves that have been improved with steps, paths, ladders, and electric lights so that sightseers can visit them in comfort. The United States National Park Service operates several caves, and there are scores of others which have state or private owners. They

CAVES IN NATIONAL PARKS AND NATIONAL MONUMENTS

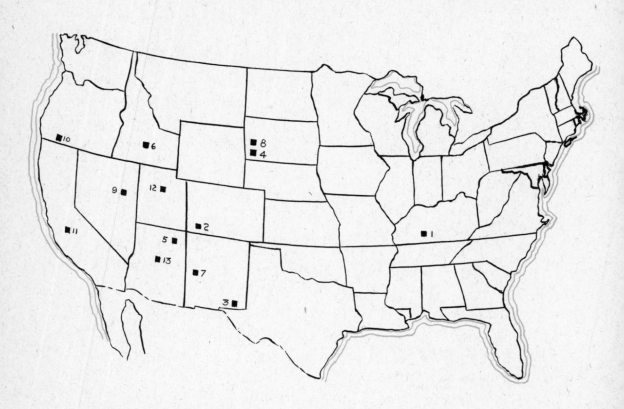

1. Mammoth Cave, Kentucky
2. Mesa Verde, Colorado
3. Carlsbad Caverns, New Mexico
4. Wind Cave, South Dakota
5. Canyon de Chelly, Arizona
6. Craters of the Moon, Idaho
7. Gila Cliff Dwellings, New Mexico

8. Jewel Cave, South Dakota
9. Lehman Caves, Nevada
10. Oregon Caves, Oregon
11. Pinnacles, California
12. Timpanogos Cave, Utah
13. Walnut Canyon, Arizona

are no longer what cavers call "wild," or untouched, caves. They have been changed enough to be safe and easy for tourists to see. They are very interesting, and are a good introduction to the underground world. No special equipment is needed in visiting them, though it is best to wear comfortable walking shoes and to carry a sweater or jacket, as the temperature underground may be colder than you expect.

Real spelunkers and speleologists like wild caves best, however, for they are a whole new world waiting to be explored. From wild caves geologists, men who study the history of the earth through its rocks, have learned much about how the earth is formed. Sometimes a river has sliced deep into a cave and has cut sharply down through its walls. Then, just as if the earth were a giant layer cake, its rock layers can be seen, with the oldest rocks on the bottom. Men who can read the cave's clues can discover much from these rocks.

Cave country is a network of underground streams which suddenly appear on the surface and just as suddenly disappear again. Cave rivers have a way of mysteriously disappearing under a cave wall, running under a mountain, and out into a valley. Men who study water supply in these areas may learn much by tracing the courses of underground rivers and learning also about the rise and fall of the underground water level.

As has already been explained, archaeologists, the scientists who study ancient ways of living, have found that caves in some places are real underground museums. They contain beautiful drawings and many of the tools and implements of the early inhabitants.

Scientists who study water and minerals or plant and animal life have only begun to learn about the many fascinating things there are underground. But most of all, caves are full of unguessed adventure and excitement. That is why so many people find that spelunking is a wonderful hobby.

CAVE ADVENTURE

In the summer of 1954, eleven adventurous spelunkers, including three women, set out to explore Schoolhouse Cave in West Virginia. Its entrance had been visited many times and the upper cave had been thoroughly explored. Parts of it had been given such imaginative names as "The Judgment Seat," "The Thunderbolt Room," "The Great Gallery," and "The Pendulum Pit."

But the explorers wanted to get down to a lower level

of the cave called "Grind Canyon," 350 feet below the surface of the earth. After an easy start the going soon became difficult. The spelunkers had to go through a waterfall, and underground water is almost always chillingly cold. Finally the spelunkers came to a deep hole. By dropping small rocks into it and counting the time that went by before they hit the bottom, the cavers knew that the downward shaft was a long one. They fastened their ropes and started slowly lowering themselves into the pitch darkness which was lighted only by the flame from lamps fastened to their hard metal hats. That downward climb was about 120 feet — about the height of a 12-story apartment house! Finally the lower cave was reached, and the spelunkers explored it thoroughly. They were in Schoolhouse Cave for 21 hours!

These people were expert spelunkers. It is wise to remember, however, that even though they all had a great deal of experience they spent a whole day beforehand in testing their equipment and getting ready for the trip.

Even more difficult and exciting was a cave expedition made near Grenoble, France, in 1954. Spelunkers there knew of a series of connected caves that went far below the surface of the earth. A group set out to go down as far as possible and to break the world record for underground depth travel if they could. The caves were very wet, and the temperature deep underground was almost icy cold. Before they started, the explorers greased their bodies as long-distance swimmers do, to help them keep warm. And they wore warm clothing topped by waterproof suits. Down and down and down they went, slowly lowering themselves by swinging ladders into yawning holes. They waded through almost freezing streams; climbed over huge rocks on the caverns' floors; and squeezed their way through narrow crevices.

They were 2,313 feet below the surface of the earth when they came to a waterfall which roared down for 52 feet and completely filled the cave passage. But even this did not

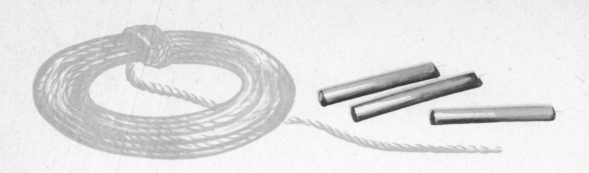

stop the spelunkers. They placed a boom out over one side of the falls, hung a ladder from it, and went on downward. When they had started on their trip, a heavy rain was falling. They knew that water would seep through the ground and swell the underground streams and that they might be caught in the cave by a flood. They went on down to 2,471 feet — far enough to break the previous world record for depth of underground travel — then hurried safely back to the surface. Two weeks later they returned to the cave and went down to break their own record by reaching a point 2,963 feet underground — more than half a mile beneath the surface of the earth.

Of course, trips like this are only for very experienced cavers. But there are all kinds of caves, large and small, easy and difficult to explore. Beginners start with simple, walk-in caves, and, as they learn the skills of spelunking, go on to harder ones. There is a cave to suit the skill of almost everyone.

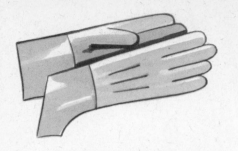
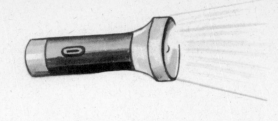

BE CAREFUL

Whether the cave is hard to explore or easy, a real spelunker is always careful. Careless exploring can be dangerous. If lights fail, there is risk of falling into a hole or a deep pool of water. Without proper care there is a possibility of getting lost. Weak or worn ropes may break. Loose rocks may be dislodged and injure a person. Sudden rains on the surface may swell an underground stream so that it fills a cave and makes drowning a danger.

Good cave explorers know of all these risks and guard against them. Real cavers understand how important it is to have proper equipment and to obey the simple safety rules of spelunking. They are:

1. *Never* explore a cave alone. Always take at least one other person with you, preferably an experienced spelunker if you are new at cave exploring.

2. *Always* be sure that someone on the surface knows what cave you are in.

3. Wear a hard hat, as protection against falling rocks or bumping your head.

55

4. Never stand at the bottom of a shaft and look upward. Even the smallest falling rock can injure a person seriously.

5. Be sure that *each person* has with him three kinds of light. One or two kinds of light may fail, and it is absolutely impossible to see in cave blackness. Take an ordinary flashlight with spare bulbs and batteries; a candle, with matches wrapped up in waterproof material; a carbide lamp which fits onto a helmet. This lamp is similar to those used by some miners. In it water drips slowly onto a solid chemical, carbide. This makes acetylene gas, which burns with a bright flame. Take refills in the form of carbide, and water in a plastic flask.

6. Before entering a cave, check all equipment to be sure it is in good condition.

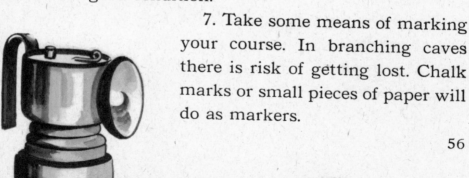

7. Take some means of marking your course. In branching caves there is risk of getting lost. Chalk marks or small pieces of paper will do as markers.

56

8. In going up and down steep and difficult places, be sure that the person climbing is attached to a safety rope which his companion secures to a firm anchoring place. Use flexible ladders (like rope ladders) for straight up-and-down climbing, but also use the safety rope.

9. Watch underground streams. If they suddenly start to rise, go up to the surface at once.

10. Always be alert and never take foolish chances.

Proper equipment is necessary in cave exploring. Clothing need not be expensive, but it must be comfortable and it must be suitable for the rough treatment it will receive. Correct shoes are very important. Cave explorers do not try to make do with a pair of old street shoes. Those will slip on wet places and they will not support the ankles. Tennis shoes have too thin a sole, and sharp rocks underfoot will cut through them and hurt the feet. Stout leather boots or those with rubber lower parts are best. Whatever the shoe, it should have a non-skid sole.

57

The other important piece of clothing is a hard hat. Some hats come with a brim in the front only. Others have a brim all round. There should be a bracket to hold a lamp; and a chin strap.

As to the rest of the clothing, there should be durable pants such as blue jeans or a coverall; a sweater or sweat shirt; work gloves; a knapsack that is easy to remove when a person is crawling through low, tight spots; and a complete change of clothing to be put on when the spelunker comes out, as he is likely to be soaking wet as well as muddy.

Other equipment includes the three kinds of light already mentioned, with extra carbide and water for the lamp, and spare bulbs and batteries for the flashlight; a canteen of drinking water; a bar or two of chocolate, and other easily carried food if this is to be a long trip. Someone in the group should have a first-aid kit. If this is a deep cave and climbing will be necessary, there should be safety ropes and a flexible ladder made of rope or wire. Ropes on a rope ladder should be protected from sharp rocks. Otherwise they will soon wear through.

So many scientists are finding caves full of new and helpful information, and so many ordinary people have discovered that caves are fun to explore, that a society for cavers has been formed. It is the National Speleological Society. Its office is located at 3047 Columbus Street, Arlington, Virginia.

One of the society's important jobs is to do everything possible to keep caves in an unspoiled state and to preserve whatever lives and grows in them. The society also gathers new information about caves, maps them, and teaches people how to explore caves safely. It has many members, all interested in the adventure they find underground.

You too may be interested in spelunking. As a hobby it is hard to beat. You are a beginner, however, so be sure to start with an easy cave, and be sure that an experienced spelunker goes with you. And remember, good cavers always obey the safety rules.

There are many fascinating things about caves aside from their unusual beauty. You might even discover something new all by yourself. But whether you make any discoveries or not, you will have a wonderful time trying. Happy spelunking!

CAVES FAMOUS IN HISTORY AND LEGEND

Near the banks of the Tiber River in Italy is the Lupercal Grotto. According to legend this cave was once the home of a wolf. One day she saw a box at the edge of the river and dragged it ashore. In it were twin baby boys, named Romulus and Remus. The wolf adopted them and brought them up in her cave. When Romulus grew up, he founded the city of Rome near the cave that had been his home.

According to an ancient Greek myth, Polyphemus was a giant with one eye. He lived in a cave where he also kept his sheep. When the Greek Odysseus was sailing home from the Trojan War, he was captured by Polyphemus. Although Odysseus put out the giant's one eye, he could not escape from the cave. When Polyphemus let his sheep out to graze, he sat at the mouth of the cave and felt the backs of each one to make sure Odysseus did not ride out. At last Odysseus got away by clinging to the belly of a ram, where Polyphemus could not feel him as he rode by.

King Philip, chief sachem of the Wampanoag Indians, was the son of Massasoit, a friend of the early New England settlers. When Philip's tribe became discontented with its treatment by the white men, the sachem could not hold his followers in check. War with the settlers followed, with bloody massacres. On a hill near Farmington, Connecticut, is Philip's Cave. At the mouth of this cave King Philip often sat, overlooking the Connecticut Valley spread out below and directing the Indians as they attacked the colonists.

A FEW WORDS USED IN CAVING

anthodite—a fragile, flowerlike limestone formation sometimes found in airtight cave chambers

bacon or **bacon strip**—two-colored flowstone sometimes found on cave walls or ceilings, so called because it somewhat resembles a slice of bacon

cave—a natural hollow, chamber, or room, or series of chambers or rooms, beneath the surface of the earth, usually totally dark

cave formation—mineral shapes formed on the walls, ceiling, or floor of a cave by the accumulation of minerals from dripping or flowing water

cave pearls—small limestone balls sometimes formed in cave pools

cave system—all the passages and rooms underground in a given area

caver—a person who explores caves scientifically or as a hobby

cavern—a cave

chamber—a large space in a cave, differing from a cave room because a chamber has only one connection with other parts of a cave. See *room*

column—a cave formation made by the joining of a stalactite and a stalagmite

curtain—a cave formation made by water dripping through a narrow crack and making a hanging sheet of limestone

dead cave—a cave which has stopped growing and changing because it contains no water

drapery—a curtainlike formation made by the joining of a row of stalactites

dripstone—any cave formation that is formed by dripping water

flowstone—any deposit left on the walls or floor of a cave by a film of flowing water

gypsum—a mineral sometimes found in caves

61

helictite—a type of stalactite that bends sideways or upward instead of hanging straight down

ice cave—a cave formed of ice in a cold climate, or a cave in which ice forms and remains throughout most of the year

lava cave—a cavity or tube formed when liquid lava runs from underneath a solid outside layer of lava

limestone cave—a cave formed in limestone

live cave—a cave which continues to be changed by the action of dripping or flowing water

room—an enlarged portion of a cave, different from a chamber because it has more than one connection with the rest of the cave

sandstone cave—a cave formed in sandstone, often through erosion by wind-blown grit

sea cave—a cave made by the action of waves on a rock cliff at sea level

shaft—an up-and-down, vertical passage at the entrance or inside a cave

speleology—the scientific study of caves

speleologist—a person who makes a scientific study of caves

spelunker—a person who explores caves as a hobby

spelunking—the exploring of caves as a hobby

stalactite—a deposit left by the evaporation of mineral-bearing water dripping from the ceiling of a cave

stalagmite—a cave formation made by a mineral solution dripping onto the floor of a cave

troglodyte—a person who lives in a cave

typhlomolge—a species of cave-dwelling salamander, pearl white with red gills

water table—the underground level below which the ground is thoroughly soaked with water

wave cave—a cave formed by wave erosion

wind cave—a cave formed by the erosion of wind-blown grit on rock

INDEX

animals, cave..................26-35
anthodites 18-19

"bacon strip" formation...........19
Bat Cave 41
bats.........................27-28
beetles, cave 34

Carlsbad Caverns...............22
cave paintings 1-7
cave pearls 20
Caves Famous in History and
  Legend 60
cocorite palms.................37
crickets, cave 33-34

"dead" caves 13-14

equipment 57-58

Fingal's Cave 22-23
fish, cave 33
formation, cave 8-20

glossary 61-62
Grenoble caves...............52-54
gypsum flowers...............19

Haute-Isle 40
helictites 18

ice caves 8, 10-12

Lascaux cave 4
lava caves 8, 9-10
limestone caves.............8, 12-13

"live" caves 13
Map of National Caves 48
Mendelssohn, Felix 22-23
Mesa Verde 41-42

National Speleological Society 59
Neanderthal men..............44
Nickajack Cave 21

oilbirds 29

Peking man..................44
plants, cave 36-38

rivers, cave..................49-50
Roche l'Eveque..............39-40

safety rules 55-58
salamanders 29-32
Schistostega osmundacea 37
Schoolhouse Cave 51-52
stalactites 15, 17
stalagmites 15-17
stone waterfalls 20

temperatures, cave 23-24
troglodytes 39-43
types of caves 8-12
Typhlomolge 31-32

Waitomo caverns 35
wave caves 8, 9
"wild" caves 49
wind caves 8

I wish to thank all those people and institutions which have encouraged me in writing this book. The National Speleological Society lent me books from their library; many members offered help and advice, particularly Mr. John Spence, who offered suggestions concerning the illustrations, and Dr. Charles E. Mohr, who read the manuscript. Dr. Brian H. Mason of the American Museum of Natural History also made many helpful suggestions. Many institutions and individuals in foreign countries were also helpful, particularly Dr. Gamard of Montoire-sur-le-Loir, who took the trouble to prepare for me a history of the troglodytes of the Loir Valley. My thanks also to Dr. J. Manson Valentine, who first interested me in caves many years ago, and especially to Minard Hamilton, whose constant help has been essential in the preparation of this book.

—The author